anoe slalom ★ cricket ★ cycling ★ diving ★ football ★ gymnas

ockey ★ netball ★ para-athletics ★ para-swimming ★ para-t

nis ★ rugby 7s ★ rugby league ★ snowboard cross ★ soccer ★ sur

swimming ★ tennis ★ water polo ★ wheelchair racing ★ wheelc

nis ★ aerial skiing ★ alpine skiing ★ athletics ★ beach volley

boxing ★canoe slalom ★ cricket ★ cycling ★ diving ★ footba

nnastics ★hockey ★ netball ★ para-athletics ★ para-swimmin

a-table tennis ★ rugby 7s ★ rugby league ★ snowboard cros

cer ★ surfing ★ swimming ★ tennis ★ water polo ★ wheelc

ing ★ wheelchair tennis ★ aerial skiing ★ alpine skiing ★ athle

beach volleyball ★ boxing ★canoe slalom ★ cricket ★ cyclin

ing ★ football ★ gymnastics ★hockey ★ netball ★ para-athle

para-swimming ★ para-table tennis ★ rugby 7s ★ rugby leagu

wboard cross ★ soccer ★ surfing ★ swimming ★ tennis ★ w

The A to Z of Who I Could Be

CHLOE DALTON
illustrated by KIM SIEW

ALLEN&UNWIN
SYDNEY • MELBOURNE • AUCKLAND • LONDON

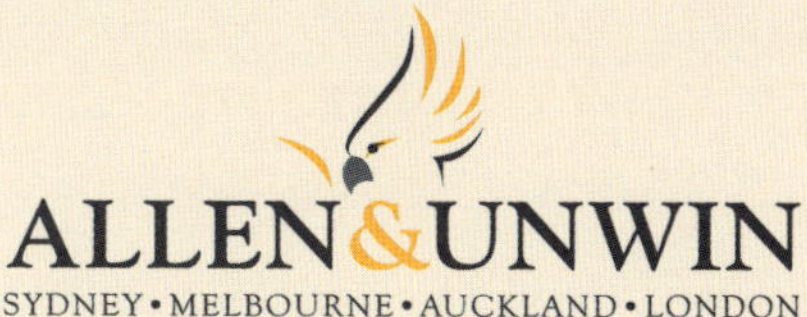

For my niece, Romi,
may you see your idols everywhere you look – CD

For Audrey – KS

A note from Chloe

As a kid, when the Olympics and Paralympics came around, my brothers and I would battle for the best spot on the couch to sit and yell at the top of our lungs cheering on Anna Meares, Louise Sauvage and Nova Peris as they raced around their tracks. I still remember the feelings of disappointment when the Games ended. Besides those four-year cycles, I didn't see my idols on TV screens or in the newspaper, I didn't hear about them on the radio, or read about them in books.

In 2020, I founded **the [female] athlete project** – Australia's fastest-growing women's sports platform, with a mission of increasing the visibility of women in sport.

This book features 26 of Australia's top athletes – Olympians, Paralympians and world champions. To all the little kids sitting on the couch watching their idols on TV, this book is for you.

Chloe Dalton x

Proud Ngaragu woman Ash absolutely blitzed the tennis world with three Grand Slam singles titles. She was the second Australian woman to reach #1, a position she held for an impressive 114 consecutive weeks!

Belle is an Australian snowboarder who competes in snowboard cross, shredding her way to three Winter Olympics, a World Cup victory, and a 2021 World Championships title in the team event.

A B C D E F G H I J K L M N O P Q R S T U V W X Y Z

Aussie beach volleyball player Taliqua is a two-time Olympian who won silver in Tokyo in 2020. She was the first Indigenous Australian volleyball player to represent her country at an Olympic Games. Incredible!

A seven-time Paralympian (wow!), Danni has competed at the Paralympic Games since 1996 – both in wheelchair tennis and para-table tennis. Among her accolades are two Paralympic medals and 10 Australian Open titles.

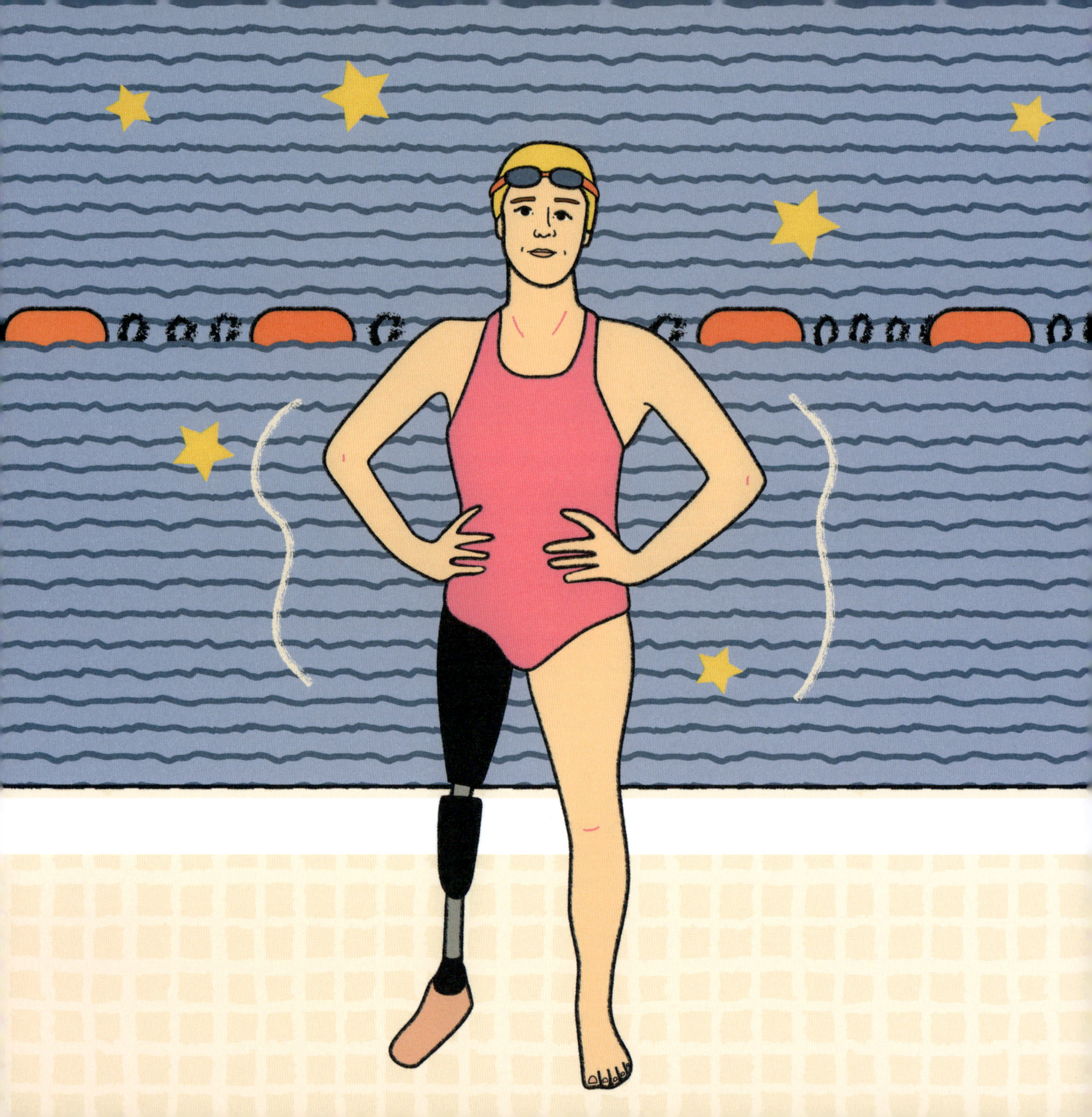

OAM

In 2021 four-time Paralympic swimmer Ellie Cole became Australia's most decorated female Paralympian of all time, with 17 medals to her name – six of which are gold. Legendary.

Professional soccer player Caitlin became the youngest Aussie to ever have played at a FIFA World Cup in 2011 when she debuted at just 16. A two-time Olympian, Caitlin's epic skills have seen her play over 100 games for the Matildas.

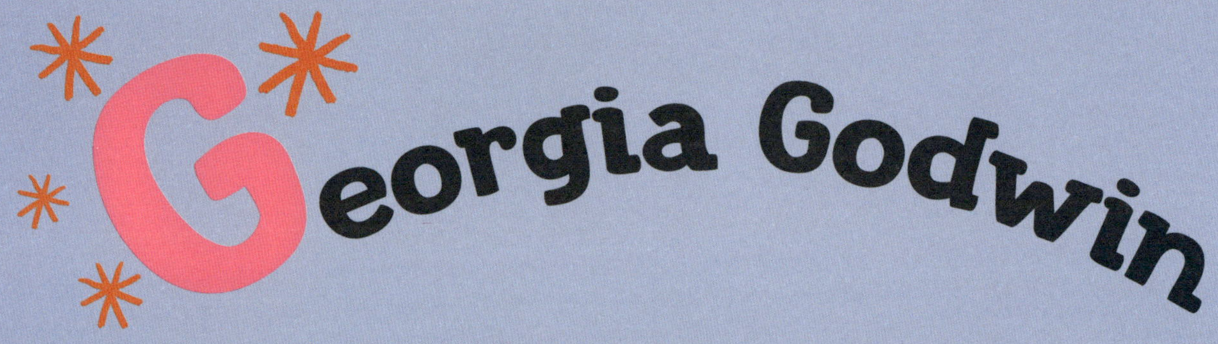

Georgia Godwin

Georgia is an artistic gymnast who represented Australia at the Tokyo 2020 Olympics, as well as clinching two gold medals at the Birmingham 2022 Commonwealth Games (equalling the most ever won by a female gymnast). She truly stuck the landing!

An AFLW player named on the All-Australian team four times, Tayla is also an Australian female middleweight and super-welterweight champion boxer (solid flex!). Her media portrayals have opened conversations around female athleticism.

Two-time Paralympian Isis is an Australian sprinter, Gold Coast 2018 Commonwealth Games gold medallist and five-time Paralympic medallist in the T35 classification as an athlete with cerebral palsy. All before the age of 21 – remarkable!

Jessi Miley-Dyer

In 2006 Jessi became the first World Surf League World Junior Champion. Fast forward to 2023 and she's now Chief of Sport for the World Surf League. Inspirational!

Steph is an absolute hockey-playing dynamo who has represented Australia at the Tokyo 2020 Olympics and both the Gold Coast 2018 and Birmingham 2022 Commonwealth Games as part of the silver medal-winning teams.

Aerial skier, five-time Winter Olympian and Vancouver 2010 Olympic gold medallist, Lydia became the first woman to land the quad-twisting triple somersault in 2014, leaving an exceptional mark on the sport. What a star!

The most successful female track cyclist in the history of the World Championships (with 11 titles!), Anna is also Australia's most decorated Olympic cyclist – with six medals across four consecutive Olympics. No biggie!

OAM

The first Indigenous Australian to win Olympic gold (with the Hockeyroos in Atlanta in 1996), Nova was an icon even before her transition into sprinting and, later, politics as the first female Indigenous senator.

Having competed at the Tokyo 2020 Olympics as well as being a Commonwealth Youth Games champion, Bendere is an absolute force to be reckoned with in her pet event, the 400 metres.

At 16, Ellyse debuted for both the Australian cricket AND soccer teams. In 2020, she was named the ICC Women's One Day International, T20 International, and overall female player of the decade. She's unstoppable!

An Olympic gold medallist, Commonwealth Games silver medallist and two-time World Series Champion for the Australian Rugby 7s, Alicia became a mother to daughter Matilda before returning to the sport.

Madison de Rozario OAM

Four-time Paralympian and wheelchair racer Madison won gold in the 800m T53 and Marathon T54 categories at the Tokyo Olympics in 2020. In 2021, she became the first Australian woman to win the wheelchair event at the New York Marathon. An unmatched champion!

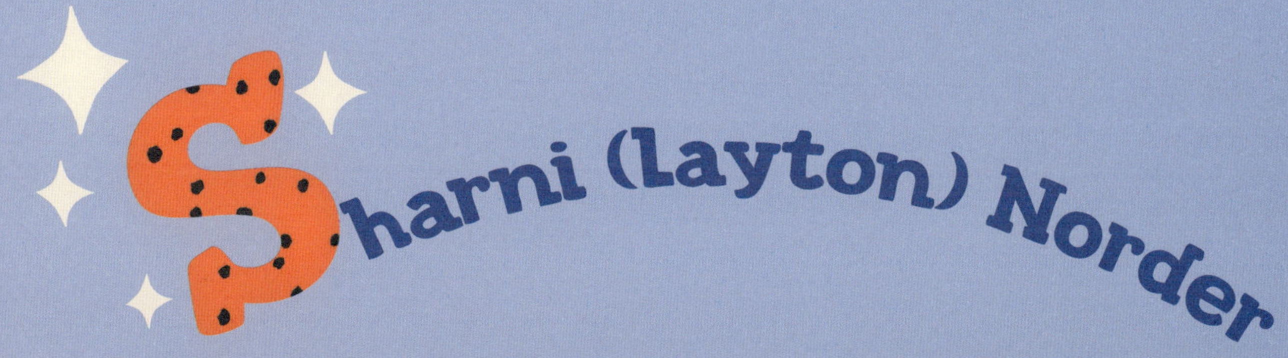

With two golds at the Netball World Cup and a gold at the Glasgow 2014 Commonwealth Games sitting in the trophy room already, Sharni then joined the AFLW where she was named in the All-Australian team in 2020.

An incredibly decorated swimmer, Ariarne's victory over reigning champion Katie Ledecky to take gold in the 400m freestyle at the Tokyo 2020 Olympics had the entire nation on their feet. Aussie Aussie Aussie!

A B C D E F G H I J K L M N O P Q R S T U V W X Y Z

A proud Baradha woman, NRLW star Tamika has played with the Indigenous All Stars, dominated the field for QLD in the State of Origin, and is currently signed to the Newcastle Knights. Triple threat!

An AFLW player for Carlton, Darcy has been named in the All-Australian team twice. In 2022, they became the first AFLW player to kick 50 goals. Literally goals.

A B C D E F G H I J K L M N O P Q R S T U V W X Y Z

Enduring diving superstar Melissa won silver at her first Commonwealth Games at just 13 years old. She is a four-time Olympian with a silver and bronze medal, and a three-time Commonwealth Games gold medallist.

A B C D E F G H I J K L M N O P Q R S T U V **W** X Y Z

At the age of just 28, Jess became the most successful paddler of all time. A three-time Olympian, she won gold at Tokyo 2020 in the C1 canoeing event.
She is unrivalled!

In an unforgettable Sydney 2000 Olympics moment, Yvette scored the winning goal to take gold for Australia in the women's water polo with only 1.3 seconds left on the clock. Iconic!

Australia's most internationally successful alpine skier, Zali won bronze in slalom skiing at the Nagano 1998 Olympics, and took gold at the World Championships in 1999. She is now an independent MP.

A B C D E F G H I J K L M N O P Q R S T U V W X Y Z

1996

Nova Peris

Becomes the first Indigenous Australian to win an Olympic gold medal in Atlanta.

1998

Zali Steggall

Wins bronze in slalom skiing at the Nagano Olympics.

2000

Yvette Higgins

Scores the goal that wins gold for Australia in the year water polo debuts at the Sydney Olympics.

2004

Danni Di Toro

Wins bronze in the Athens Paralympics wheelchair tennis women's singles.

2006

Jessi Miley-Dyer

Becomes the inaugural World Surf League World Junior Champion.

Melissa Wu

Wins silver at her first Commonwealth Games at just 13 years old.

2011

Caitlin Foord

Becomes the youngest Matilda to debut at a World Cup at just 16 years old.

2012

Anna Meares

Defeats rival Victoria Pendleton to win Olympic gold in the sprint.

2013

Jess Fox

Wins gold in the inaugural C1 class at the ICF Canoe Slalom World Championships.

2014

Lydia Lassila

Becomes the first woman to land a quad-twisting triple somersault.

Sharni (Layton) Norder

Wins a Commonwealth Games gold medal for netball.

2015

Steph Kershaw

Makes her debut for Australia playing a test match with the Hockeyroos.

2016

Taliqua Clancy

Becomes the first Indigenous Australian volleyball player to represent Australia at an Olympic Games.

2017

Bendere Oboya

Wins gold in the 400m at the Commonwealth Youth Games.

2018

Isis Holt

Wins gold at the Gold Coast Commonwealth Games in the Women's 100m T35.

Alicia (Quirk) Lucas

Wins her second World Series title with the Aussie 7s team.

2019

Tayla Harris

Is famously photographed mid-kick in an AFLW match and calls out online trolls.

26 athletic achievements from Awe-inspiring to amaZing

Belle Brockhoff

Wins the World Championships snowboard cross team event.

Ellie Cole

Becomes Australia's most decorated female Paralympian.

Ariarne Titmus

Beats Katie Ledecky to win the 400m freestyle at the Tokyo Olympics.

Madison de Rozario

Becomes the first Australian woman to win the wheelchair event at the New York Marathon.

Ash Barty

Wins the Australian Open women's singles title.

Darcy Vescio

Makes history becoming the first AFLW player to kick 50 goals.

Georgia Godwin

Wins two gold medals at the Birmingham Commonwealth Games.

2020

2021

2022

2023

Ellyse Perry

Is named the ICC Women's ODI Cricketer of the Decade.

Tamika Upton

Secures longest deal in NRLW history when she signs a five-year contract with the Newcastle Knights.

About the

During a Covid lockdown in 2020, Chloe Dalton started **the [female] athlete project** from the garage of her parents' home as a space to share the stories of incredible female athletes: Olympians, Paralympians and world champions – athletes who should be household names recognised across the nation, but who had not received the media coverage they deserved.

Chloe and **the [female] athlete project** team noticed a distinct lack of up-to-date news highlighting the achievements of women in sport.

[female] athlete project

In 2021 they launched podcast 'the wrap', covering everything happening in women's sports news. **the [female] athlete project**'s online audience has since grown to over 50 000 followers, a community who are engaged and passionate about the growth of women in sport.

Until female and gender diverse athletes receive equal coverage in the media, and are recognised by their achievements, not by their gender, **the [female] athlete project** will keep sharing the stories of those blazing the way.

Find them on Instagram **@thefemaleathleteproject**

About the Author

Chloe Dalton is the founder of **the [female] athlete project** and is one of Australia's few triple sport elite athletes. After playing basketball in the WNBL with the Sydney Uni Flames, Chloe transitioned to rugby, where she debuted for the Australian Rugby 7s team in 2014. At the Rio 2016 Olympics, Dalton won gold with the Australian Rugby 7s team and was awarded an Order of Australia Medal for Service to Sport. She was also recognised as Australia's top Rugby 7s player in 2017, winning the Shawn Mackay Medal. Chloe then crossed codes again to Aussie Rules, making her debut in 2019 for Carlton in the AFLW. She was recently named Runner-Up in the Carlton Best and Fairest Awards for the 2020 AFLW season. Chloe currently plays AFLW for the GWS Giants.

About the Illustrator

Kim Siew is an illustrator and mural artist who lives and works on Gadigal Land. Although not an athlete, she does love to scale large walls with a brush in hand to paint her drawings onto grey buildings around the city. She has illustrated several books and art games and is currently experimenting with short-form comics. When not drawing, you will find her wandering laneways for inspiration with her loyal Jack Russell cross, Alfie, reading a graphic novel on a park bench with a croissant in hand, or channelling her excess energy through boxing (where she is quite content to sit at sparring level).

A portion of the proceeds from the sales of this book will be donated to the Nova Peris Foundation.

First published by Allen & Unwin in 2023

Allen & Unwin
Cammeraygal Country
83 Alexander Street
Crows Nest NSW 2065
Australia
Phone: (61 2) 8425 0100
Email: info@allenandunwin.com
Web: www.allenandunwin.com

Allen & Unwin acknowledges the Traditional Owners of the Country on which we live and work.
We pay our respects to all Aboriginal and Torres Strait Islander Elders, past and present.

A catalogue record for this book is available from the National Library of Australia

ISBN 978 1 76118 042 2

For teaching resources, explore www.allenandunwin.com/resources/for-teachers

Illustration technique: digital illustration

Cover and text design by Hana Kinoshita Thomson
Cover illustrations by Kim Siew and Hana Kinoshita Thomson
Set in 20 pt Brandon Grotesque by Hana Kinoshita Thomson

This book was printed in June 2023 by C&C Offset Printing Co. Ltd, China.

1 3 5 7 9 10 8 6 4 2